The Wonderful World of Food

by Wiley Blevins

raintree

a Capstone company — publishers for children

Engage Literacy is published in the UK by Raintree.
Raintree is an imprint of Capstone Global Library Limited, a company incorporated in England and Wales having its registered office at 264 Banbury Road, Oxford, OX2 7DY – Registered company number: 6695582

www.raintree.co.uk

© 2018 by Raintree. All rights reserved. No part of this publication may be reproduced, stored in a retrieval system, or transmitted in any way or by any means, electronic, mechanical, photocopying, recording or otherwise, without the prior written permission of Capstone Global Library Limited.

Editorial credits
Karen Soll, editor; Lisa King (cover), Kazuko Collins and Charmaine Whitman, designers;
Wanda Winch, media researcher; Katy LaVigne, production specialist

Image credits
Alamy Stock Photo: Jim West, 25; Capstone: Karen Soll, 22; Dreamstime: Radu Brotoiu, 34; Getty Images Inc: AFP/SEYLLOU, 21; iStockphoto: JohnnyGreig, 27, kali9, 4–5, SolStock, 46; Newscom: Reuters/Edgar Su, 16–17, 18–19 (background), Reuters/Toshi Maeda, 42–43; Shutterstock: Adisa, back cover, 1, Adrianasilvaxavier, 37, Agenturfotografin, cover (top right), Alena Haurylik, cover (bottom middle), Alison Hancock, 33, B Amonrat, 38 (t), bigjom jom, 41, ch_ch, cover (top left), ChameleonsEye, 8–9, Colorfulworld86, 13 (greenhouse), Dervin Witmer, 7 (b), Eddie J. Rodriquez, 11, irra_irra, 31, Jakob Fischer, cover (tmr), John Bill, 14–15, Kateryna Ovcharenko, 29, kathayut kongmanee, cover (br), Lucky Business, cover (tml), Nancy Kennedy, 7 (t), Nina Osintseva, cover (bl), pablofdezr, 18 (inset), Peter Zijlstra, 40, P-fotography, 39, PILart, 12–13 (background), Sebastian Knight, cover (ml), successo images, 44–45, Taiga, lettuce leaf background, teekaygee, 12–13 (weather icons), Thomas Francois, 47, Vdovina Elena, 13 (garden elements), Withan, 38 (b)

21 20
10 9 8 7 6 5 4 3 2 1

The Wonderful World of Food

ISBN: 978 1 4747 4657 1

Bibliography
pp. 22–25: Judith Rubleske. Personal Interview. 25 July 2016.

p. 30 Anger, Judith, Immo Fiebrig, and Martin Schnyder. "Edible Cities: How Urbanites Can Grow Their Own Food." *The Telegraph*. 13 December 2013. http://www.telegraph.co.uk/gardening/howtogrow/10514160/Edible-cities-how-urbanites-can-grow-their-own-food.html

Printed and bound in India.

Contents

Where people get food 4

Desert farming 8

Terrace farming 14

Vertical farms 16

Urban gardens 20

Urban beekeepers 26

Growing food in and around the house . . . 30

Unusual fruits and vegetables 36

Other unusual foods 42

Glossary 47

Index 48

Where people get food

Imagine you're sitting in a restaurant. The waiter brings your meal. You dig into a plate of steaming food. Yum! But have you ever wondered where that food came from? The rice might have come from Asia. It could have spent weeks on a boat to get to you. The lettuce might have been grown at the other end of the country. It could have spent a long time in a lorry to get to you. The cherry tomatoes might have been grown closer to home. They could have been picked today from the restaurant's windowsill garden. Food comes from farms and other sources all over the world.

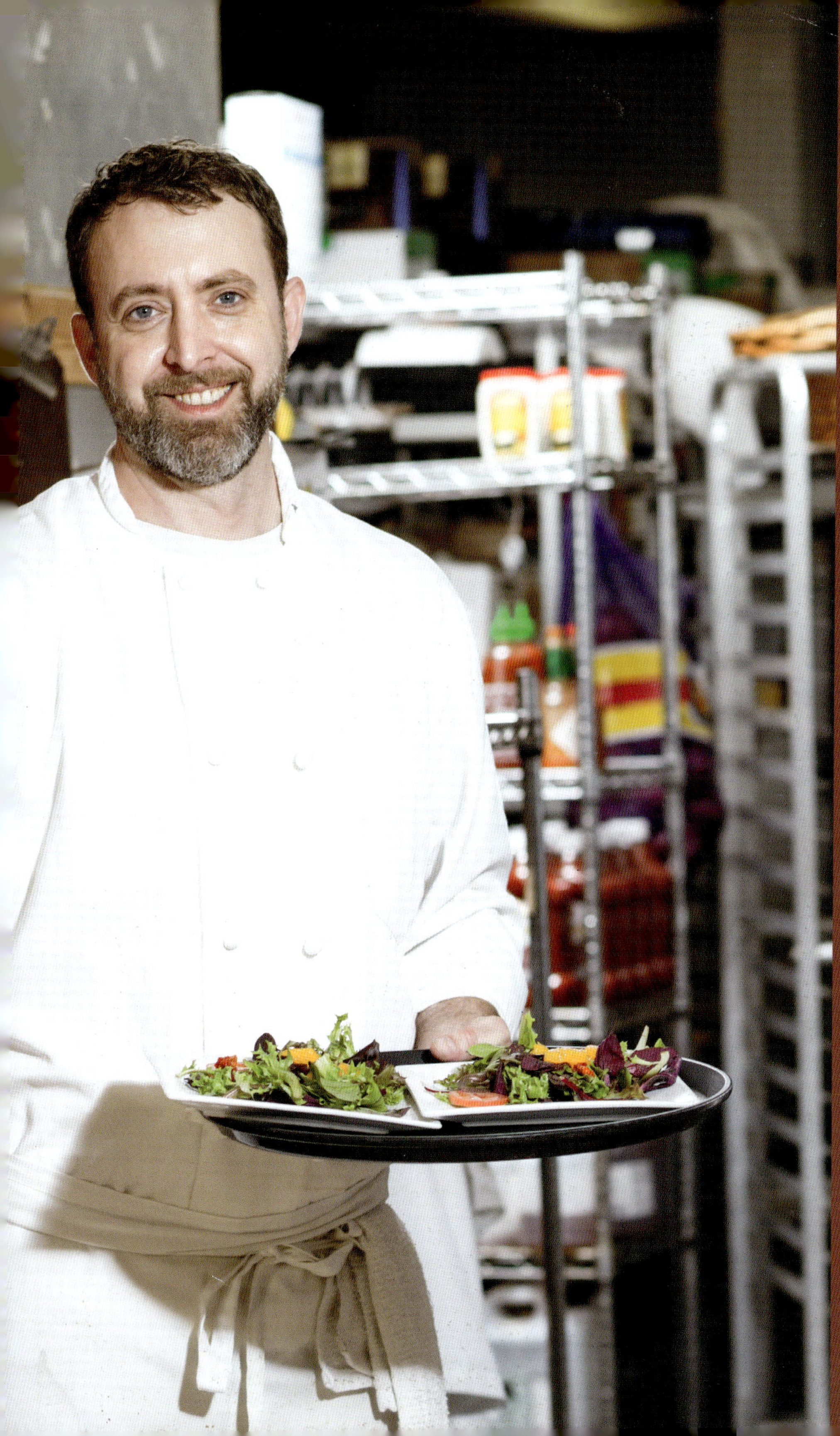

When we think of farms, we picture flat, wide-open fields. We think of golden wheat fields or we imagine orchards full of fruit trees. Farming involves using the soil to grow crops that are then used for food. Farmers also rear animals for food, such as chickens, cows and sheep. Farms come in many sizes, and they can be located in some surprising places.

orchard

farm

Desert farming

You wouldn't think of deserts as good places for farming. Plants need lots of water to grow, and deserts get very little water. So how do people who live in deserts grow the food they need? It begins with *irrigation*.

Irrigation is the way farmers get water to their crops. There are many ways to do this. One way is to use large sprinklers, which can run on timers. The sprinklers give the plants the water they need.

Another way to water crops is called *drip irrigation*. Small, thin pipes are placed all over a desert farm. Water drips from the pipes onto the plants. The water only drips close to the plants' roots. This gives the plants water where and when they need it.

Desert farming can be found all over the world. This farm is in Israel.

Many desert farms use complex irrigation systems. The desert farms in the Imperial Valley of California, USA, grow much of the country's winter vegetables. More than 75 crops are grown here, such as spinach and onions. Farmers use pipes to get water from the distant Colorado River. Now this desert blooms with plant life all year. Animals, such as cattle, sheep and catfish can be found here as well.

Irrigation can also happen in semi-*arid*, or semi-dry, places. During the dry season near the Ord River in Australia, the river dries up to just a few ponds.

This water irrigation pipe is used in the dry farmlands of southern California, USA.

A *dam* was built to help make sure that the area received water all year round from excess water collected during the rainy season. The dam helped create Lake Argyle. Water from this *reservoir*, or lake where water is stored, is sent to *local* farms. Today, the lake still provides water to farms.

Desert saltwater greenhouses

Crops need fresh water to grow. Rain is fresh water. Fresh water is also found in lakes and rivers. Some parts of the world only have access to salt water. Salt water is found in oceans and seas, and it can harm plants. When plants *absorb*, or take in, salt water, it can stop them from growing and can kill them. So what do farmers do if most of the water they have is salty? In the Sahara Desert in Africa, they've come up with a solution. Here farmers build saltwater *greenhouses*, or warm buildings where plants can grow.

Diagram of a saltwater greenhouse

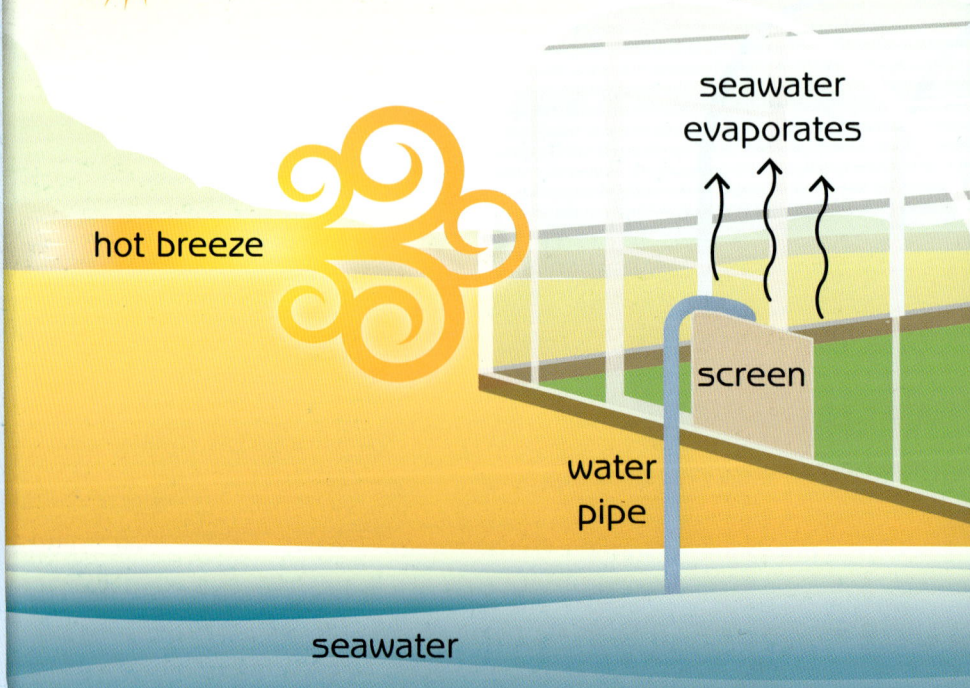

seawater evaporates

hot breeze

screen

water pipe

seawater

How does this type of greenhouse work? The cold salt water is piped into the greenhouse. It flows down a screen inside the building. As the cold water hits the hot air inside, it begins to *evaporate*. That means it turns from liquid water to a *gas*, or vapour. Little water droplets start to form everywhere.

The water vapour in the air collects on the plants as little droplets of water. This gives the plants the water they need to live. But there's one extra bonus. When the water evaporates, the salt stays behind on the screen. It doesn't harm the plants.

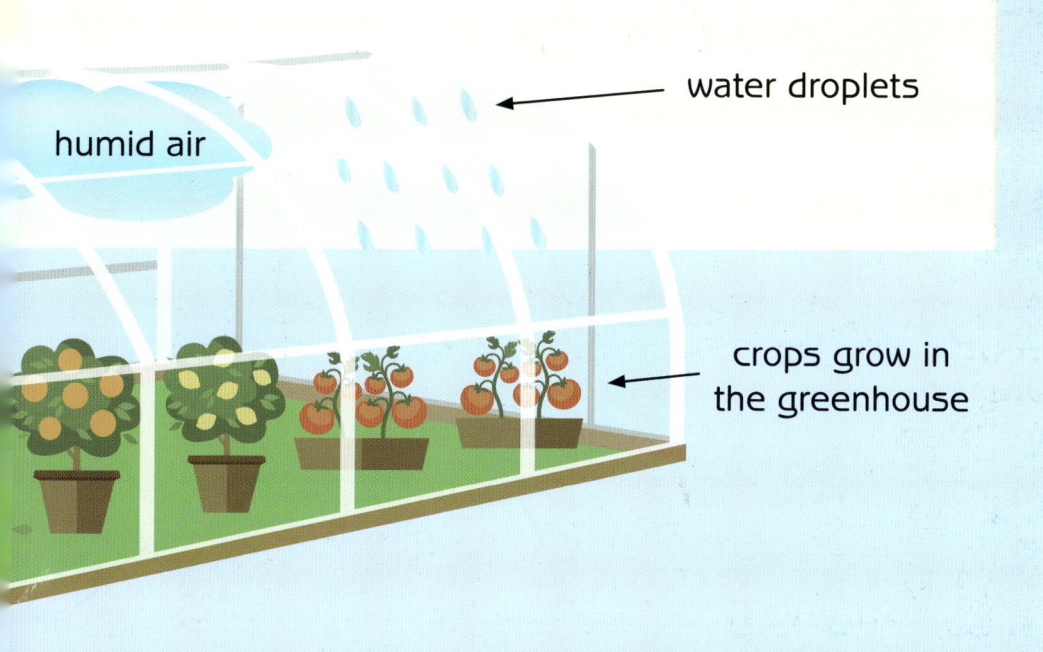

humid air

water droplets

crops grow in the greenhouse

seawater

Terrace farming

Most crops are grown on flat land. It is easier to grow crops and use farm machines when the land is flat. But in some parts of the world, growing crops on flat land is not something that can be done. These places have sloping hills or tall rocky mountains. Sheep can live on some hills, but hills are not always easy to grow crops on. What can farmers do?

This terrace farm can be found in Vietnam. It's used to grow rice.

They cut fields into the sides of the hills. It's like carving stairs up the side of a mountain. These fields are called *terraces*.

You can find terrace farms all over the world. Farmers in China and Southeast Asia use terraces to grow rice. In South America farmers grow potatoes and corn on their terrace farms.

Vertical farms

Who says a garden has to be in a field? Who says a farm has to be on the ground? Not *vertical* farmers. Picture fields of plants stacked on top of each other like shelves in a drawer. That's a vertical farm.

There are lots of good things about vertical farms. They are often indoors, take up little space and use less water than other kinds of farms. And they can be grown in cities, where there is little land for farming. They can be found all over the world, including Asia, the United States and even in the UK.

How do vertical farms work? These farms have a special water system. The water is piped in, floor by floor. Some also use artificial, or fake, light to act like sunlight. Others don't even use soil. One university in the UK plants crops in water with fish living in it. *Waste* from the fish helps the plants grow. And because the plants are often inside buildings, the farmers don't have to worry about the weather. If a blanket of snow covers the ground outside, it doesn't matter. Too much rain? It's not a problem because the plants are inside and away from harsh weather.

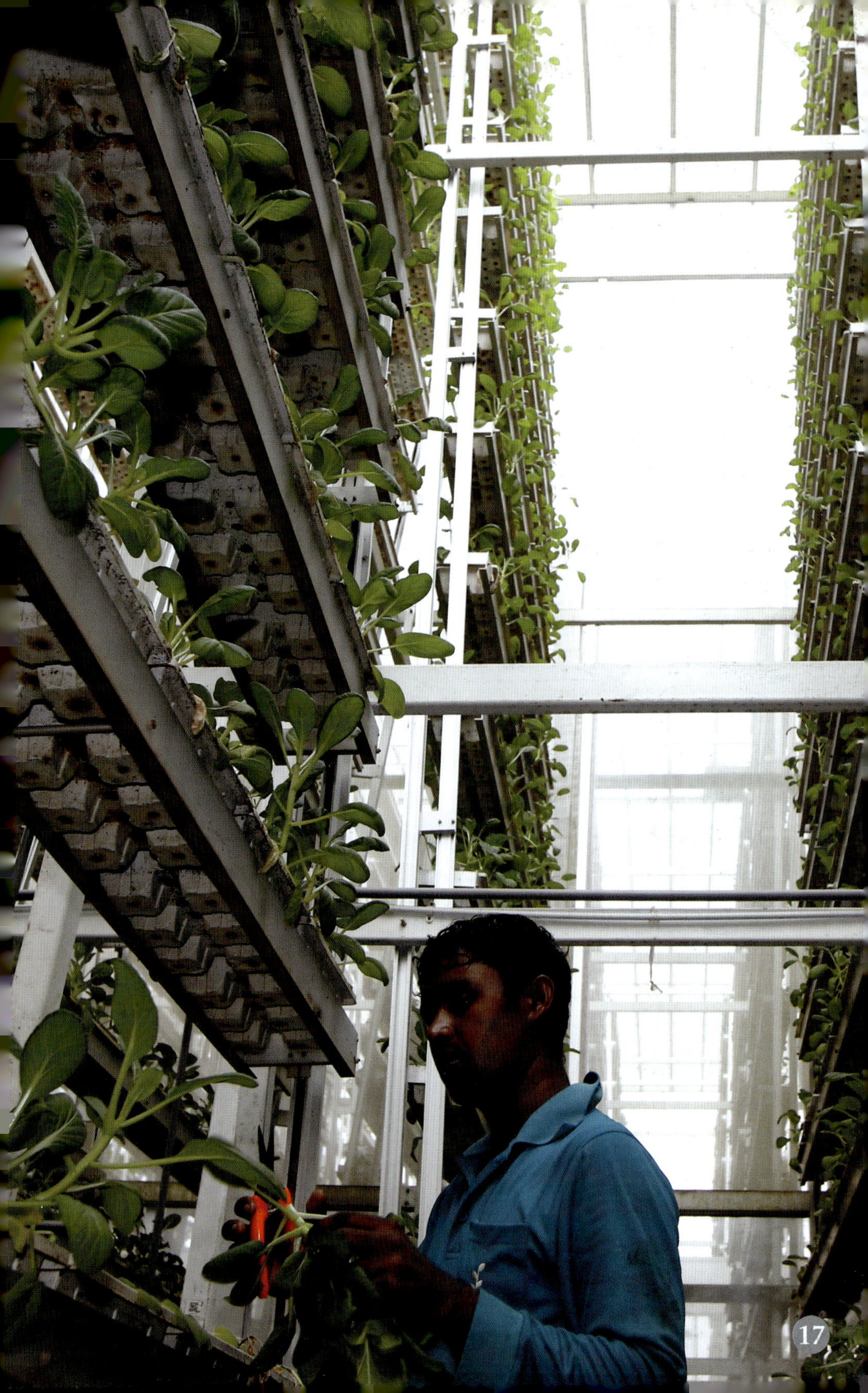

Map of Asia

Japan

Singapore

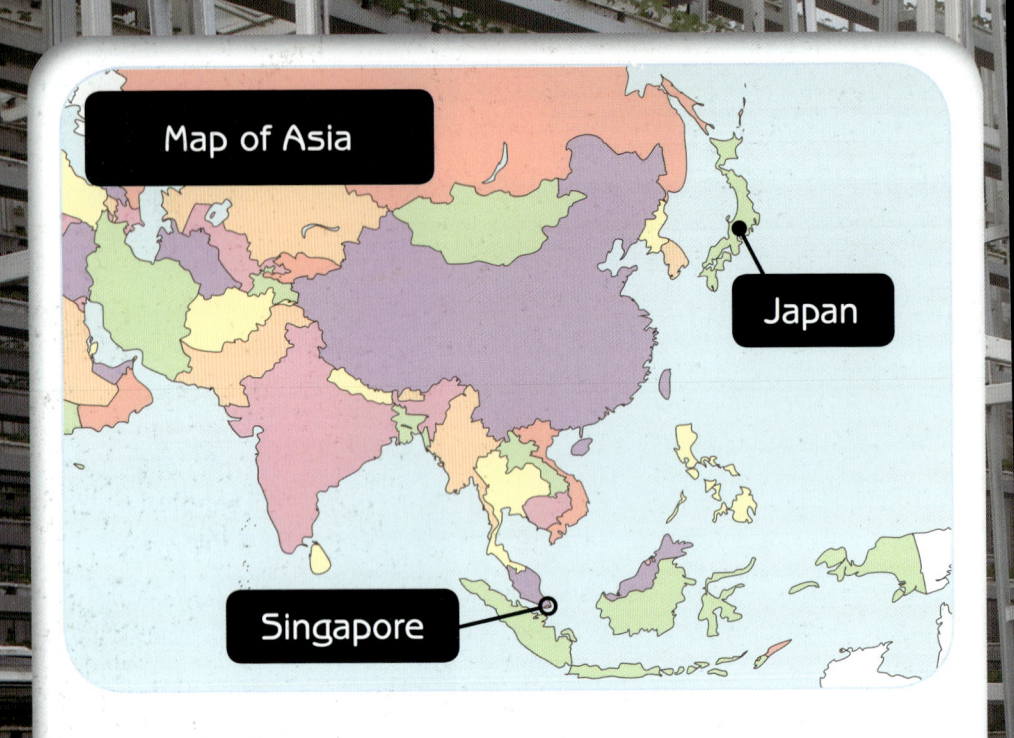

One vertical farm in Japan was built after an earthquake. The earthquake triggered a tsunami. This wall of water struck Japan and destroyed local farms. The farm helped to feed the people living there. It could produce more food than a more common type of farm.

Singapore is home to a large vertical farm. The farm is housed in a giant steel building. It has more than 120 towers of plants reaching nine metres high. This farm helps grow more food locally. When food is grown locally, people don't have to *import*, or bring in, as much food from other countries.

This vertical farm in Singapore grows lots of vegetables.

Urban gardens

Cities are often filled with many different types of building. It can be hard to find wide-open spaces, so farming is less common. To help these communities, people grow *urban* gardens. They can be vegetable gardens that neighbours tend together. These gardens make a city community more beautiful. They can also provide a lot of food. Some urban gardeners even rear animals, such as chickens.

In New York City, one group has built or improved more than 80 community gardens. This group works with communities to change vacant, or empty, spaces into gardens. A second group provides a programme for children in the city. They plant, water, weed, grow and *harvest* vegetables. Then they sell their food at a local farmers' market.

Groups like these are popping up all over the world. The United Nations has a group that helps people in Senegal, Africa, start community gardens. These gardens are grown on roofs and in empty spaces.

A small one-square-metre garden can produce 30 kilograms of vegetables every year. That's enough food to feed an entire family for one year. There's even some left over to sell!

This woman is gardening on a rooftop in Dakar, Senegal.

Interview with a community gardener

Q: What gave you the idea to create community gardens?

A: One day I was thinking about my neighbour. I thought a garden would be a great way to help him and many other neighbours in need.

Q: What do you grow in your gardens?

A: We grow beans, sweet peas, onions and squash. We also grow peppers, herbs and spinach. We plant a lot of easy-to-store vegetables.

Q: What happens to all the food you grow?

A: One third of the food grown is shared by the people who work in the gardens. One third is sold to local restaurants. The money is used to cover costs for the gardens for the next year. The last third is given away to a local food bank. The food bank helps to feed people in need in our community.

Q: How did you learn about gardening?

A: I've always loved gardening. I first learned about gardening from my family. Now I read as much as I can about how plants grow. I also try new ways of growing plants in my gardens. Did you know that some plants grow better together than others? And they don't all grow at the same time of the year. I've made a planting schedule to help me plan when to plant and harvest the plants.

Q: Why are gardens so important?

A: They do more than provide food. Working in nature helps people. I have noticed that the fresh air and pride in growing a garden helps people to feel better. I like that.

Q: How have volunteers heard about your gardens?

A: Some newspapers write about the gardens. I also attend events and talk about them. I teach an Earth Friendly Eating programme at the local library. We put up posters with contact information, too.

Q: Your gardens also help the soil. Why is that important?

A: With these kinds of gardens, we grow healthy food while keeping the soil and environment safe. I don't use harmful *chemicals* to get rid of pests in the gardens. There are plants we can grow that will help with that. I also grow some plants as food for the soil. They give *nutrients* back to the soil. The more you give back to the soil, the better the soil will be for new crops to grow.

Q: What goals do you have for your gardens?

A: We want to make the gardens a jewel in our city. We hope they will serve as a model for other communities.

Urban beekeepers

As well as growing food, urban farmers are also rearing bees. Beehives are sprouting up on rooftops and in small gardens around many cities. Why? Bees make honey. Bees are also important to nature. They are needed to *pollinate* many plants. The bees move pollen from plant to plant, which makes new plants grow.

This beekeeper is making sure the beehives are healthy.

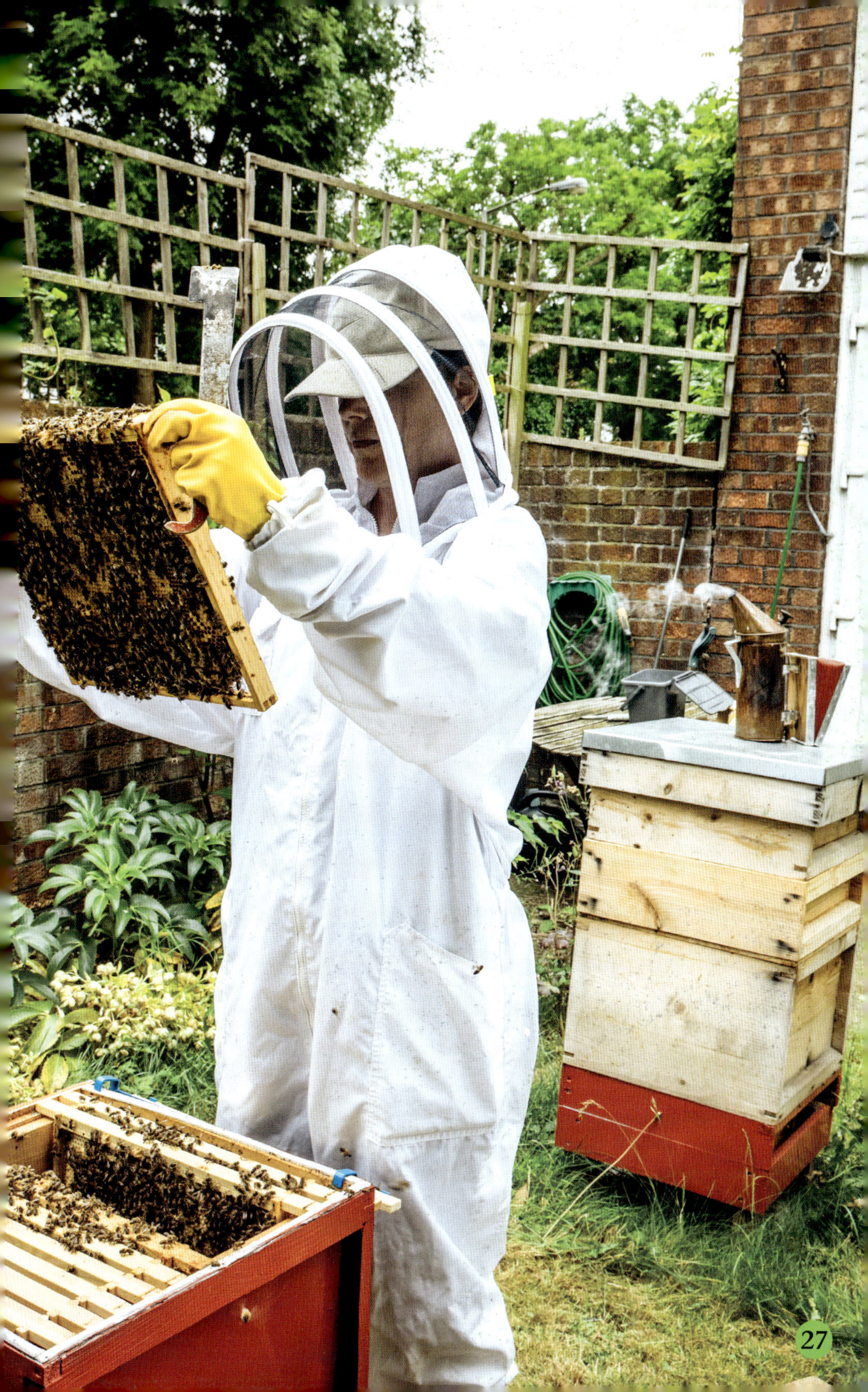

City bees produce a lot of honey. Scientists believe it's because they have many sources of food in the city. But sometimes that has a downside. Bees eat lots of sweet things. Bees feed mainly on the sweet nectar found in plants. But when the bees get their sweet food from somewhere else, the results can be shocking.

In one city the bees feasted on a red food dye from a nearby factory. The dye changed the bee's honey. Instead of making the normal brownish honey, their honey was red!

Bees feed on nectar found in flowers.

Growing food in and around the house

You don't have to leave your house to be a farmer. You can grow food on your rooftop or windowsill. You can even grow food on a shelf. People all over the world are growing food in and around their homes.

In Tokyo, Japan, one farmer grows melons on nets. These nets are like small vertical gardens and are a great way to grow food when you don't have a garden. In Vienna, Austria, a woman has turned her apartment into a garden. She puts pots on her windowsills and on shelves. She even grows tomatoes indoors. The vines climb over her window like a curtain. In her words, "I also like knowing where my food comes from."

Tomatoes can be grown indoors. They just need to have enough light and heat to grow properly.

In Michigan, USA, one man grows plants in empty buildings. He uses old items that have been thrown away. With this rubbish, he makes raised plant beds.

In some cities roof gardens are more common. In fact, when a new building is built in Paris, it must have a roof garden or *solar panels*. The panels collect sunlight and turn it into electricity. These efforts help people living in cities grow some of the food they need. This also cuts down on the costs of shipping food from far away. It's better for the environment, too.

Urban rooftops are used to grow all kinds of plants. This one is used to grow vegetables.

In Switzerland some people make balcony gardens. Good soil is often hard to find, so two people have worked out a way to make their own *compost*. They use willow branches, old baskets, dust from the vacuum cleaner and worms. These things make compost, or a mixture. The compost helps make the soil better food for the plants. People also use old plastic bottles to help water the plants. They turn them upside down and pop them into the dry soil. In their gardens they grow vegetables and herbs.

A plastic bottle is used to water this plant.

Seven great plants to grow at home

Would you like to grow a plant at home? These plants are perfect for growing in small pots.

Plant	What the experts say
1. nasturtiums (flowers)	These bright plants are known as the "Queen of Edible Flowers".
2. chillies	One plant can produce 50–100 chillies, but they need a lot of sun to grow.
3. Asian greens	These leaves grow really quickly, don't need much sun and are great in salads or stir-fries.
4. runner beans	You can grow many beans in one pot, but they do need a lot of water.
5. peas and broad beans	These plants are fast and easy to grow. They take just three weeks. Plus, they need only one hour of sunlight each day.
6. tomatoes	You can grow 5 kilograms of tomatoes from just one plant. But you will need to use good soil.
7. mixed salads	This is the best crop to grow at home. Mixed salad leaves grow quickly and are packed with flavour.

Unusual fruits and vegetables

People eat fruit and vegetables every day. Bananas are the largest fruit crop in the world. Corn is the largest vegetable crop. Did you know that 7,500 different varieties of apple are grown around the world? But in some places, other fruits and vegetables are more common. Grown locally, these foods are easy to get hold of. Some of these fruits and vegetables might surprise you by their look, name or taste.

The jaboticaba tree grows mainly in Brazil. It has small black fruit that taste like grapes. People make jam and juice from the tasty fruit. The unusual thing about this fruit is that it doesn't just dangle from the tree's high limbs. The fruit grows all over the tree and the tree's trunk. From a distance it looks as though the tree is covered in big oily tears.

jaboticaba tree

durian tree with fruit

The durian tree grows in places such as Thailand and Brunei. If you walk through the forest in these countries you're likely to find this fruit tree. Why? Because it smells awful! You can smell the fruit from far away. People say it smells like rotten fish or a sewer. The smell is so bad, it's against the law to eat the fruit in public in some places. But many people love the taste.

Hala aka Puhala fruit

Travel to Hawaii and you might get to try the fruit of the Hala aka Puhala tree. This fruit looks like a starburst with many sections that spread from its middle. Its insides can be eaten raw or cooked. In Jamaica, you can eat the ugli fruit. It has rough, wrinkled, greenish-yellow skin. Ugly! But don't let the name or look keep you from trying this fruit. It tastes like a sweet tangerine. The bright pink dragon fruit will draw you in. It grows in Central America and throughout Asia. Scoop out the white, seed-filled insides and enjoy.

dragon fruit

Kiwano melon

The Kiwano melon looks like a pufferfish. It has spikes on the outside that look like horns. The melon is eaten in Africa and New Zealand. When it ripens, its insides taste like a mix between lime, cucumber and banana.

The yardlong bean is also called the Chinese long bean. Its pods can grow up to 76 centimetres long. It has a nutty flavour and is common in Asia.

yardlong beans

Other unusual foods

Cows and chickens are animals commonly reared for food. But they aren't the only animals people eat. In some parts of the world, lots of other animals are cheaper. So that's what the local people eat.

Travel around the globe and you might find people eating ants, rats or even spiders. These foods come in a rainbow of flavours, and they are packed with nutrition.

In Thailand, jing leed is a tasty treat. These large grasshoppers are covered in salt, pepper and chili powder. Then they are fried. In Japan, wasp crackers can be found. These are cookies filled with this flying insect.

rice cracker with wasps

fried silkworms

In Korea, silkworms are boiled or steamed. They are sold by street vendors, so it's easy to grab a handful of them on a city walk. In Africa insects are an easy-to-find source of protein. Stinkbugs are said to taste a bit like apples. They can be eaten alone or added to stews.

Whether you eat insects or chicken, ugli fruit or apples, most of your food comes from farms. The farms may be big or small. They may be in your own garden or thousands of kilometres away on the other side of the world. Wherever people live, they find ways to grow the food they need. So the next time you sit down for a meal, ask yourself: "Where has my food come from?" The answer might surprise you!